THE BROKEN TWO-PARTY SYSTEM

How a Multi Party System Can Restore Civility and Community to the Country

ROBERT ALEX

outskirts
press

Outskirts Press, Inc.
http://www.outskirtspress.com

ISBN: 978-1-9772-1525-3

Cover Photo © 2019 www.gettyimages.com. All rights reserved - used with permission.

Outskirts Press and the "OP" logo are trademarks belonging to Outskirts Press, Inc.

PRINTED IN THE UNITED STATES OF AMERICA

Table of Contents

Chapter One

"Let me … warn you in the most solemn manner against the baneful effects of the spirit of party."

~ George Washington, September 19, 1796.

TODAY THOSE "BANEFUL effects" George Washington cautioned us about are in full pyrotechnic display around us.

Americans today are spewing out a fiery, toxic rhetoric at each other which would make most parents blush if they heard those words coming from the mouths of their children. Friends and family have become irreparably divided, not just by "policy" disputes between themselves, but by the inflammatory invective that has publicly sprung forth from what were once only tame differences of political opinion.

And, yes, the media is standing on the sidelines fanning the flames of this divisive conflagration.

Americans need to place themselves above the current political spectrum and ask themselves what are the morally correct actions they need to take to move the country forward.

As an Eastern guru once said, "The solution to the problem is never at the level of the problem itself." The division we see and feel in the country today will not be resolved on the field of today's dishonorable politics. Our political arena will only begin to improve by voters acting on their innate moral sense, not – like too many of today's politicians — on those more selfish ideas of "what's in it for them."

Not that there isn't a great division in the country today which needs to be recognized by people so they can understand they need to change the way things now are. A 2016 Gallup poll, for instance, showed that seventy-seven percent of us, the American public, see the country as divided. That's a record high number, it claims, although the Civil War may have slipped Mr. Gallup's mind.

Political partisanship is causing the great divide in the country.

To a large degree, the dangerous flame springs from our two-party system. By its very nature, it promotes partisan politics and, almost by necessity, divides the nation.

In rancorous periods, such as our own, of intense partisanship between two recalcitrant factions, we get the "baneful effects" that George Washington predicted. In periods of the most intense partisanship, of course, we get civil war.

George Washington, as well as the rest of our Founding Fathers, were well aware of the more base side of mankind – having just witnessed the excesses of the French Revolution — and they did a remarkable job of creating a structure for their new government which protected itself from those less lofty impulses of human nature. The Constitution was created to protect its offices from the men who would hold them, and the Founding Fathers all shared a loathing for any two-party system. They knew by its nature it catered to social division.

And they were right.

The basic difficulty in any two-party system is one of structure, not necessarily of opposing political philosophies. Any binary division – such as a strictly two-party system — sets up an irreconcilable polarity between two, and only two, options: right and wrong, good and bad, truth and lies, federalists and anti-federalists. A concept only makes sense and can only be defined by knowing its opposite. Black only has meaning because of white, rich because of poor, young because of old.

Our conventional mind set is with a two valued system, and with any two valued system, friction occurs between its two polarities.

A multi-party system not only offers more points of view to choose from between those two polarities – those two political parties that have dominated American politics – but a multi-party system also offers broader political points of view for citizens to champion.

Given the acceptance tier of Overton's spectrum and Hallin's parallel sphere of consensus, the philosophies of the two major parties must fall within a certain tolerable range of acceptability for a politician to be easily elected. That phenomenon places both parties in a arbitrarily narrow position on the wider spectrum of philosophies which include notions that might be too radical or too controversial – to use Overton's and Hallin's terms – to be accepted immediately by the general public. Only over time do these broader points of view prove to have merit, and then they are incorporated into actual application by the two main parties.

In the first half of the nineteenth century, for instance, the anti-slavery advocates were too controversial to have their positions taken seriously by the two major parties, each of which catered to their own pro-slavery positions. By 1865, however, the anti-slavery viewpoint was acknowledged as the true moral stance and was validated by the 13th Amendment, which abolished slavery and involuntary servitude.

If a voter consults his own moral sense and chooses a political option that matches his integrity, then the range of new ideas available to match that moral choice will be far greater with a multi-party system. There will be a much wider spectrum of choice than our current two-party system offers. Radical or initially controversial ideas can have moral merit even if they are not options at that moment within those two acceptable, political parties.

It is only the most extreme fringe positions that are usually immoral and unacceptable. As Dwight Eisenhower said in 1956, "If a political party does not have its foundation in the determination to advance a cause that is right and that is moral, then it is not a political party; it is merely a conspiracy to seize power."

Not only does a two-party system limit voters by placing all political choices into a narrow, binary spectrum, but that two terminal structure also makes it all the easier mechanically for sparks to fly between proponents – like crossing the two poles of a car battery with a screwdriver — when only those two, binary choices are available.

Add in the "human nature" of it all and you get an emotional division that might start off as consternation between two parties, but quickly ends up at the heated peaks of incendiary partisanship that we see in the country today.

When was the last time you and your spouse started arguing about going to your in-laws or not for Thanksgiving – a seemingly innocent little polarity – but ended up in a knock down, drag 'em out fight that brought up everything from you getting drunk at your brother's wedding to her breaking off your engagement because of Billy Wildman. That escalation into an obsessive need to be right about your side of the polarity will also trigger your need to make your spouse wrong. After all, if your spouse is proven to be wrong, you have to be right.

It's the same with two political parties. It's the human nature Washington and his fellow patriots were trying so hard to design a government to avoid.

The obsession to be right and make your opponent wrong as part of a different political party has moved from the innocent rhetoric of campaign speeches and pamphlets through the more agitated, neurotic bashing of opponents, to what has become the often obsessively psychotic and vindictive rhetoric that's as toxic to our culture as all the plastic waste we've managed to dump into the ocean is to our environment. Human nature gone wrong.

With only two parties as our choice, the slide into partisan politics is a short one, just as our Founding Fathers unanimously predicted would be the case. Within a multi-party voting landscape, a wider spectrum of points of political view can stretch out between those two polarities, and human nature's need for harsh rhetoric can be diminished while the possibility of a far broader representation of popular views is increased.

To remedy the toxic division we see in our country today, only two facts need to be taken into consideration. First, there is a problem with the electoral process of government. Second, change will only be possible if people take action. That requires taking a moral stance. If one recognizes there is something terribly wrong with our system, one has a duty as a citizen to try to fix it.

When one's moral sense reveals what is wrong, one works toward what is right.

To do that we only have to take into account the tactic that history has proven to work: identify the problem and take corrective action.

We have a simple cause/effect situation. As the government fails us through two-party politics, we the people suffer. Our two-party system has become increasingly corrupt and dysfunctional and needs to be replaced with a multi-party system.

That won't happen by tomorrow at four o'clock. The two-party system has become too locked into place over the last seventy years through the growth of personal political dynasties and vested interest funding as well as by the simultaneous rigging of our voting system to make it impossible for any political parties except the Democrats and the Republicans to succeed.

We're not looking at anything as excessive as beheading Marie Antoinette here to solve these woes. We're only looking at changing the rules of a system that is not working to one with a more proportionate representation for voters and so eliminate the underlying cause of so much fiery division in our country, the two-party system.

Yes, it may be true that there are other factors to today's unhealthy partisanship – the greatest being the national media's inflaming supporters on each side of the polarity with their divide and conquer strategy to feed a sometimes unholy appetite for advertising revenue. However, the media's fanning these fires to the degree they do is only possible with a two-party system, because that basic binary polarity is needed to engage those right/wrong and good/evil impulses that out Founding Fathers cautioned us about and that seem to be a part of human nature.

Today sixty-one percent of Americans have told Mr. Gallup that they like the idea of a third major party. That's not new. The same percentage has been in favor of multi-party politics since 2007.

The question is not: do the American people want a multi-party system? The question is: how do we get it?

The question is also: how was it that our country went from our first utterly non-partisan president, who had no party affiliation – he was "just George" — in his eight years of office to the two hundred and forty years of increasingly divisive, two-party politics ever since?

Chapter Two

"There is nothing which I dread so much as a division of the republic into two great parties, each arranged under its leader, and concerting measures in opposition to each other. This, in my humble apprehension, is to be dreaded as the greatest political evil under our Constitution."

~ John Adams, Letter to Jonathan Jackson (October 2, 1780)

BY 1776 THE distaste the Founding Fathers had for political parties had become as strong as their appetite for a new political freedom.

The colonists' beef with Britain was less with the monarch himself than with British Parliament. Despite the Declaration of Independence bill of particulars listing the specific points of the ongoing acts "despotism" forced upon them by the King of England, the American colonists had long since recognized the abuses stemmed not solely from the king himself, but from the Parliament with its two-party system that the colonists had grown to fear, and abhor, as a structure within government.

The fractious behavior the colonists had witnessed by

the Whigs and the Tories in Parliament was something they wanted to avoid. That meant no political parties in their new country. The Founding Fathers recognized that even the British party labels themselves – each coined by the other party, amusingly enough — showed the bitter, make-wrong nature of any two-party system. "Whig" was a crude Scottish term for curdled milk and "Tory" an equally derisive Irish word for highway robber.

The word "party" was never used in the Constitution itself when it was signed in 1787. George Washington was elected first president in 1789 with no party affiliation and he was reelected for a second term, still with no party affiliation. The "baneful effects" of a two-party system had been avoided in the Constitution and in the first years of our new government.

The accepted axiom of the day was that a gentleman should not have to stoop to campaign for public office. Instead, as the saying went, "The office should seek the man. The man should not seek the office." Serving in a public office was seen as a trust and a selfless service toward the public good, not a profitable career. There was no separation between a man's moral stance and his political station.

The more base aspects of "human nature" were to be kept out of government's corridors. As Alexander Hamilton had written in one pronouncement that was representative of his peers' anti-party views: "We are attempting, by this Constitution, to abolish factions, and to unite all parties for the general welfare."

Thomas Jefferson had a different idea, however.

He had served as America's Minister to France and had aligned himself philosophically with the revolutionaries who would soon initiate the French Revolution. His espousal of their rallying cry *"liberte, egalite et fraternite"* can be seen to influence his writing of the preamble to the Declaration of Independence, and his appetite for a new political freedom was as strong as any of his American compatriots.

Unlike the majority of the Founding Fathers, though, he was a proponent of a two-party system. Had he not been in France during the creation of the new American Constitution, his influence for including a two-party system into the Constitution would have been stronger, perhaps even successful.

He had written to his American compatriots, "Men are naturally divided into two parties, those who fear and distrust the people and wish to draw all power from them into the hands of the higher classes and those who identify themselves with the people, have confidence in them, cherish and consider them as the most honest and safe, although not the most wise, depository of the public interests." The early binary opposition within humanity which he describes here has set forth the polarity from which sparks have been flying in this country ever since.

Although his binary view of men, and human nature, also paralleled the federalist/anti-federalist arguments of the Founding Fathers, the sentiment at home during the Constitutional Convention was to keep that polarity

– as well as the parties that might represent it – out of the Constitution itself.

Although disagreeing with Jefferson, Washington recognized him as a force to be reckoned with and he appointed him his Secretary of State as a gesture of non-factional unification. Jefferson quickly began disagreeing with Washington's ideas for a strong central government and began to undermine Washington's implementation of federalist philosophy. Washington was ready to dismiss Jefferson as his Secretary of State, but Jefferson left voluntarily. Still, Washington would not forgive him for his opposition and he never spoke to Jefferson again.

Human nature had seeped it first stain onto American politics.

With Jefferson the two-party system in America had been conceived, but it was not given a full birth until 1791 when Jefferson and Madison formed the Democrat-Republican Party to oppose the federalist polices of the government. Washington's successor, John Adams, signed into law the punitive Alien and Seditions Act in an attempt to squash Jefferson's Democrat-Republican Party, and therefore the rise of a two-party system within the country, but that effort failed.

Meanwhile, Hamilton had resigned from Washington's cabinet to put all of his efforts into the formation of another political group to protect his views and the second president's, John Adams', from the anti-federalist Jeffersonian contingent.

The nation's first two parties were now alive and well

and at each other's throats.

The first two-party election in American history came next – each faction had now nominated an official party ticket — and the campaigning became one of the most vicious and divisive in our history — although today we are giving its rancorous conflagration a good run for its money.

In that 1800 election Jefferson tied Burr in the number of electoral votes each received, and both received more electoral votes than Adams and his co-candidate, Pinckney. The House of Representatives finally resolved the tie after thirty-six contentious ballots. Jefferson became the nation's third president in 1801 and the two-party system has remained the foundation of American politics ever since.

Our system of two-party polarity had not only been given birth — and a violent one at that — but it then became officially christened with the passing of the Twelfth Amendment in 1804.

Ostensibly proposed to eliminate the problem of a tie occurring in a presidential election – like the one that had just occurred between Jefferson and Burr in the 1800 election – the Twelfth Amendment restructured the Electoral College and the country's original vote tallying method was scrubbed. During the 1796 election, federalist and anti-federalist factions had already become consolidated into two political parties, but by the rules of the original Electoral College, that presidential election resulted in a federalist president, Adams, and an anti-federalist Vice President, Jefferson. After 1804 there was only the first-past-the-post vote counting for each office, separately.

The friction between Adams and Jefferson after 1796, as president and vice president, then became the second problem, besides ties, in the election process under the Electoral College, as originally written. Watching Adam's and Jefferson's unwillingness to work together as unified leaders of the country – their own human nature unbridled — the remaining Founding Fathers' consensus was that a correction for that was also needed to the procedures of election by the College.

The Twelfth Amendment was ratified in 1804 to solve those two problems.

To prevent tie votes – but also to help ensure the election of a president and vice president from the same party – each elector now cast one vote for president and one separate vote for vice president. The House of Representatives would then resolve by ballot any elections where there was no absolute majority, with each state having only one vote for one of the top three contenders.

In the original Electoral College format, to prevent an earlier concern of electors voting in only their favorite sons from their own states, electors had to place one of their votes for someone outside their state. After the ratification of the 12th Amendment, that requirement began to favor a loyalty to party affiliation rather than loyalty to one's state.

The Electoral College had originally been conceived to facilitate elections without political parties and without national campaigns, but the 12th Amendment now provided a legislative stamp of approval for the fact of political parties – but only two of them – in American presidential elections.

Chapter Three

"America will never be destroyed from the outside. If we falter and lose our freedoms, it will be because we destroyed ourselves."

- Abraham Lincoln

ALTHOUGH THE TWELFTH Amendment helped cement the two-party polarity into American politics, in the first fifty years of the nineteenth century there were still few administrative barriers to third party presidential candidates. The finances needed to run a campaign were not great, volunteer manpower was readily available and, most importantly, there were no arbitrary restrictions to getting one's name on a ballot.

In fact, political parties printed and distributed their own ballots in those days and no candidate therefore needed to petition, as they do today, to appear on a ballot. Political parties controlled their own balloting until the late eighteen hundreds when state legislatures – controlled by the country's two major parties, of course — took over

15

the printing of standard state ballots.

Although that new state legislature control was initially proposed to stamp out the illicit buying and selling of ballots, that control also allowed state legislatures to determine the qualifications of any candidate to appear on a ballot. State legislators – who were predominantly in one of the two mainstream parties – found they had a new tool to hamper any third-party opposition to their two-party stronghold.

The country's first unwieldy, arbitrary petitioning requirements were introduced for any candidate trying to appear on a ballot, and those "rules" are still in place today as one of the greater barriers to any third party candidacy.

Despite the relative ease of multi-party candidates running in those first fifty years of the 1800's, few actually did. In the 1832 presidential election there were two third party candidates, William Wirt from the Anti-Masonic Party and John Floyd from the Nullifier Party, and their candidacies represented only the first and second official third parties to run in an American presidential election. Wirt was a single issue candidate opposing Freemasonry while Floyd represented a pro-slavery, states rights platform.

1832 was also the first year the two mainstream parties held national conventions, and these further strengthened the perceived validity of two mainstream parties as the only two worthwhile and "acceptable" choices for voters. In that election Andrew Jackson, the incumbent Democrat candidate, handily beat Henry Clay, the Republican nominee.

That year, the Anti-Masonic party had also held its own national nominating convention, giving it some authority as a third party, and even though it lost, it had drawn enough national attention and political clout to merge with what was left of the then failed Republican Party to form the Whig Party. Sixty years earlier the Founding Fathers had only derided the Brit's "curdled milk" Whig moniker, but for the next twenty years after 1832 the ironically named American Whig Party remained the chief opposition to the Democrats and the formidable second terminal to America's continuing two-party polarity.

In the 1848 and 1852 presidential elections the Free Soil party appeared on the ballot, another single issue party devoted to opposing the expansion of slavery into the western territories. This was another attempt by a third party to topple the candidates of the two main parties, and like the earlier two attempts, it was unsuccessful. It did show the potential of several alternative parties joining forces as one third party to unite their opposition to the acceptable pro-slavery platforms of the two major parties, though, and other third parties have adopted that strategy of coalition just to gain even the slight footholds they have in American politics.

That strategy may have been an important lesson to the fourth third party run in American politics by Abraham Lincoln in 1860, a run that was successful in a huge multi-party field of six parties and six candidates.

The increasingly divisive two-party factionalism between the Whigs and the Democrats from 1832 on had kept each president in that period to only one elected term. The incendiary division between pro and anti-slavery positions and state sovereignty arguments was being fanned into one final, heated, irreconcilable polarity that ultimately resulted in the southern states secession and then the Civil War.

"Honest Abe" was a moral man. His alternative viewpoint of the immorality of slavery was still outside the then "acceptable" views of 1860, but the anti-slavery moral stance of his successful re-election campaign was soon validated by the ratification of the 13th Amendment. The prohibition of slavery and indentured labor was finally accepted into the American political spectrum, and it came in through Lincoln's third party back door.

By 1860 the political landscape of acceptability in America was fractured enough that six parties held national conventions, a true multi-party election. The northern Democratic Party (the original Jeffersonian Democratic-Republican Party), newly founded Republican Party of Lincoln, and four other parties were able to field their presidential candidates.

Lincoln won only forty percent of the popular vote, but he became the first presidential candidate to understand the importance of campaigning for the electoral vote. That strategy, along with the strong coalition he had created to form his new Republican party, elected him for a second term.

He became the one and only third party candidate ever to win an American presidential election.

In 1864 Lincoln ran his reelection campaign again as a third party candidate, this time as the nominee of the National Union Party, and won the election by both fifty-five percent of the popular vote and ninety-five percent of the electoral vote. The Civil War was still raging and no electoral votes were counted from any of the eleven states that had joined the Confederacy.

Lincoln's views opposing slavery and his ideas on how to overcome it illustrate a third party's ability to bring into the Overton's "acceptable" range a viewpoint that is moral, but not politically viable, initially. Although a lifelong opponent of slavery, Lincoln avoided the political categorization of Abolitionist – not a politically expedient position to hold – and opted instead for a long term solution to slavery, the 13th Amendment proposed during his second term, rather than the more volatile solution offered by John Brown and his political Abolitionist allies.

Overton's acceptable range still included many pro-slavery elements – otherwise eleven southern states would not have seceded – but it took a third party candidate, operating from a purely moral stance, to bring into the real world an acceptable implementation of that moral stance.

Perhaps nowhere else in American history has the value of a third party candidate been shown as an agency to set the country right by reaffirming the inalienable rights of its Constitution.

The last half of the nineteenth century saw only one short lived third party, the Populist Party, in the 1892 election, but after the turn of the century a flurry of third party presidential candidates arrived on the scene as minority, sometimes radical, points of view came to the forefront in American politics. Although no candidate was successful, each party helped realign the political landscape in ways not possible through the "normal" two-party system.

Only Teddy Roosevelt's Progressive and Eugene Debs' Socialist Parties achieved any great visibility in presidential elections, and they also each illustrate the potential of a minority viewpoint moving toward the acceptable. Debs took seven percent of the popular vote, but his local supporters won a hundred and fifty local elections for Socialist mayoral candidates. His Socialist party's demise came from its refusal to merge with any other third party viewpoint to gain political strength.

Roosevelt took twenty-seven percent of the popular vote in the 1912 election, and his ability to do that well against his own Republican Party and their Democratic opponent depended to a large extent on his ability to merge other third party viewpoints into a unified coalition force. Although a less divisive climate than pre-Civil War factions, by the turn of the century the Progressive Era had ushered in minority representation for women suffrage, the eight hour work day, a social insurance program, and – perhaps the most "moral" viewpoint of all – the dissolution of what Teddy called "the unholy alliance between corrupt business and corrupt politics."

He made that the first task of the statesmanship of the day.

Not surprisingly, that particular plank of his platform

did not sit well with those entrenched leaders of the Republican and Democratic parties who recognized the threat to their own livelihood in Teddy's Square Deal.

Only at the state and local levels did third party candidates begin to be successful during that Progressive Era. There were governors elected from the Progressive, Reform, Farmer-Labor, Populist, and Prohibition parties and at one point the United States had six hundred mayors elected from the Socialist Party, in part because the local socialist parties had taken on the causes of the suffragette movement and the need for stricter child labor laws.

Then, in 1913, Congress ratified two amendments, the 16th and 17th, which effectively squelched any threats to Roosevelt's "unholy alliance," primarily the two ruling parties. Combined, these two amendments first made a senator's election dependent on a popular vote – thus ensuring their loyalty to a political party, not to a particular home state – and second, established a national tax that could be used for the unlimited funding for expansion of a federal government. Elected officials would now be paid very well.

These amendments together made it possible for many long term personal political dynasties we now see within the US Congress and shifted the motivation to be elected from solely service to one's country to the more selfish goal of a lucrative career.

Being a mainstream Republican or Democrat was the first criterion for any politician's entry into this exclusive new club.

Teddy Roosevelt's unsuccessful Square Deal turned into his distant cousin's successful New Deal in 1933 after Franklin demonstrated his own expertise in merging a coalition of minority viewpoints – just as Teddy had done – that might otherwise have ended up under the leadership of rival third party candidates. With the relatively unlimited funding now available to the government after the 16th Amendment's new tax revenues, FDR was also able to build big city political machines by financing millions of relief jobs and promising billions of dollars in entitlement programs. Our two-party system was effectively reduced to a single party Democratic system for his four terms as president.

Third party politics were sparse after that. In 1948 Strom Thurmond launched his Dixiecrat Party for a third party run at the presidency, but he won only two percent of the popular vote because his political agenda was too far from the "acceptable" range of American political sensibility.

Only three other third party presidential candidacies have occurred since Thurmond. George Wallace ran with the American Independent Party in 1968, another pro-segregationist, one issue Southern party, and won almost fourteen percent of the popular vote. John Anderson was the National Unity Party candidate in 1980 and he managed to gather about seven percent of the popular vote after qualifying for all fifty ballots, raising enough money to mount a national campaign and being invited by the League of Women Voters to participate in the televised debates. In

1992 and 1996 Ross Perot ran first as an independent than as the Reform Party candidate. In the 1992 election he received almost nineteen percent of the popular vote and his was therefore the most successful third party candidacy since Teddy Roosevelt's in 1912. Unlike Thurmond and Wallace, however, Perot received no electoral votes.

Although there have been other third party presidential campaigns mounted — John Hospers', for instance, the first of many Libertarian candidates – the two major parties have since World War II created a monopoly through erecting enough financial, balloting and debate barriers to preserve their dominance and prevent any serious alternative political viewpoints or parties from competing with them.

Chapter Four

*"Nothing could be more ill-judged than that intolerant spirit
which has, at all times, characterized political parties."*
~ Alexander Hamilton, October 27, 1787

"WE MUTUALLY PLEDGE to each other our lives, our
fortunes, our sacred honor." This was the promise by the
Founding Fathers in their Declaration of Independence.

They understood the necessity of personal sacrifice as
leaders of the country. They understood that leadership
is selfless, never self serving, and that the freedoms that
are most important, most lasting, are those that are greater
than the individual.

That is the level of morality the country was founded
on and that was the selfless standard the Founding Fathers
aimed for and adhered to. They were moral men who
sometimes may have held differing opinions as to the best
way to serve the public good, but they agreed unanimously that serving the public good was their true office.

Thomas Jefferson may have been contentious, but

only in advocating for his ideal of what was the greatest public good. He pledged as fully as his compatriots his "life, fortune and sacred honor," words that he himself had composed.

"Let the office seek the man, not the man the office" was the Founding Fathers' credo for electing selfless officials devoted to the good of the country and its citizens. Personal ambition was the aspect of "human nature" they were so wary of, and the one they most wanted to avoid in any public office.

Today there is a lot of "human nature" masquerading as government.

Personal fame, fortune and power have too often replaced the high moral stance the Founding Fathers had intended for public office holders, and the subsequent corruption we have in government today manifests itself in a divisive political rhetoric that obscures the need to act in the greatest public good. It also hides the personal power structures that have developed in our two-party system.

Today's career politicians – a term that itself would have repulsed our Founding Fathers — have effectively ensured there can be no third party challenge to the two-party system that now so safely harbors their own personal political dynasties.

That has not always been the case. In fact, personal political dynasties are a recent phenomenon, made possible by the 16th Amendment's guarantee of lucrative political careers through federal tax funding. Add to that the *quid pro quo* relationships that career politicians have developed with political action committees, lobbyists and covert business funding and the moral motivation of elected office holders to serve selflessly has too often been diluted and even washed away by the attraction of power and wealth that is now available through personal political dynasties.

Only after the national emergencies of the Depression and World War II had been handled could the political landscape begin to spawn these long term personal political strongholds. Of the twenty-two longest serving U.S. Senators, with terms ranging from thirty-six to fifty-one years, all but two occurred after WWII, and only one of those began before the taxation of 1913. Of the fifty-seven longest serving U.S. Representatives, with terms ranging from thirty-six to fifty-nine years, all but one served virtually his whole term after WWII.

Those seventy-nine career politicians themselves comprise fifteen percent of our Congress. That number does not include all those other politicians who have so far served less than thirty-six years, but are well on their way to their fourth decade of building a personal dynasty.

The morality of these modern politicians is more tainted than in any earlier time in our nation's history, and that ethical stain is coincident with the rise of these personal dynasties.

Our Congress has three levels of justice they can apply to members found guilty of illegal or immoral acts. Expulsion is the highest disciplinary action available to Congress, censure of Senators is the next echelon, and reprimand of U.S. Representatives is the next lower order of disciplinary justice.

Of all the Representatives reprimanded by Congress, there is an almost equal number of Democrats and Republicans. However, there was never the need for an official reprimand before 1976. Corruption is a modern phenomenon.

Of all the Senators who have been censured, there are more Democrats than Republicans. Many censures had been made for senators supporting the Confederacy, of course, and most of the other earlier censures in our history were for "unparliamentary language." This is itself and indication of a stricter application of moral standards in the country's early days. If "unparliamentary language" were applied for censure today, there would be a long line of senators sitting on a bench awaiting their disciplinary hearings.

Since 1979, however, all the censures of U.S. Senators have been for financial improprieties. Personal dynasties gone awry.

In U.S. history only three congressmen have actually been expelled, the most severe disciplinary action available, for any activity other than joining the Confederacy. One of those three was expelled in 1797 for inciting the Indians to support the British.

The two other expulsions have occurred in the last forty years, and they were for the financial crimes of bribery and racketeering. Again, money over morality.

In our early days it was definitely morality over money.

In 1789 a congressman received fifty cents per day for his service. By 1815 his compensation had risen to $1,500.00 per year, but that's still only the equivalent of $20,000 in today's dollars.

The average annual salary for a U.S. Congress member today is $174,000. The median net worth of those serving in Congress is more than a million dollars. The top net worth is currently 357 million dollars.

Perhaps only one congressman was expelled for bribery, but the question remains: when does quid pro quo actually become bribery. Even if favors don't reach the level of illegality, how often do they transcend the boundaries of morality. Speaking fees of fifty thousand dollars per talk and up, offers of lucrative ad hoc teaching positions, appointments as salaried members of corporate boards of directors all contribute to a politician's net worth and skirt the moral borders of quid pro quo.

Most long term, personal dynasty Congress members have a net worth far greater than they could have achieved even if they had saved every penny of their salary. One quarter of those elected to Congress say they earn more income from outside investments than their $174,000 annual salary.

The average congressional campaign today costs close to ten million dollars, but the individual candidate does not need to come up with any of that out of his or her own pocket. Since 1943, political action committees have been able to help finance political campaigns. Since 2010, Super PACs have been able to do more of the same, but with a virtually unlimited cap on individual contributions.

Compare this to the legislated restrictions on matching federal campaign financing for third party candidates. They must first raise $5,000.00 in twenty different states for initial federal matching funds, and then, in the federal election, they must have received five percent of the popular vote in the previous election to be eligible for federal funding. These rules, legislated by those two-party politicians in power, have effectively barred candidates without the deepest of pockets from even being able to run.

And the money needed to have a chance to win against these career politicians is an even greater barrier.

In the 2018 election cycle, the 2,395 SuperPACs that now exist received 1.5 billion dollars in donations and spent 808 million dollars on individual campaigns.

A donor is not allowed to give a million dollars to an individual campaigning politician, but he is allowed to contribute that much to a SuperPAC that then invests it in that politician's campaign. That's a million dollar opportunity for a less than moral – although completely legal, it seems – *quid pro quo.*

"You can't get rich as a politician unless you're a crook" was Harry Truman's terse hyperbolic take on quid pro quo back in the nineteen fifties. Yes, only two senators have actually been expelled, recently, for bribery and racketeering, but their two crimes are only the visible, illegal big brothers of the far more frequent, if hidden, immoral *quid pro quo.*

Political *quid pro quo* results in less corporate

competition, more embedded power centers, greater income gaps and in general less value for the American people, and the American people know that. This shadowy aspect of American politics helps create the gaps between politicians and the public they are supposed to be serving, and those gaps span the polarities and fill with the divisive sparks that are keeping our culture aflame.

Our exclusive two-party system has narrowed the playing field of those who can and do rule by rewarding them with wealth and power. Today there is little of the selfless humanitarian satisfaction that our Founding Fathers sought from the offices that should only serve the good of those they represent.

Today it is too often the man who seeks the office, and it is the office itself that has suffered as our republican democracy moves toward becoming a covert oligarchy of a few powerful politicians.

Chapter Five

"The alternate domination of one faction over another, sharpened by the spirit of revenge, natural to party dissension, which in different ages and countries has perpetrated the most horrid enormities, is itself a frightful despotism."

~ George Washington, September 19, 1796.

TO BE TRUTHFUL, "republican democracy' is a bit of an oxymoron.

In a republic, a constitution protects certain inalienable rights of all the populace and those rights cannot be taken away by the government itself. In a democracy, the majority of the populace is not so restricted. The majority can rule the minority.

The Declaration of Independence asserts the inalienable rights of all, and the Constitution is the Founding Father's attempt to provide a governmental structure to prevent the majority holding sway over the minority. Unfortunately, because of the limitations of the two-party system, we now have the minority of these personal political dynasties able to impose their will on the majority.

A multi-party voting system would help restore the power of both the majority and the well represented minorities – when voted in appropriately and through the standard constitutional electoral processes — to register their views with the greater population, just as the Founding Fathers intended. The barriers of finances, balloting and debate participation that have been imposed by the oligarchy within today's two-party system have created a monopoly for the Republican and Democratic platforms.

The strength of diversity, championed by the Founding Fathers, through a broad and proportional representation of political views is only possible through a multi-party system. A multi-party democracy may be preferable to an exclusively two-party republic.

Our traditional two-party system had evolved in an earlier Anglo-Saxon period when society was simpler and there were more limited voting rights. It was not a period of political or cultural diversity. Encyclopedia.com notes that "All in all, traditional two-party systems, which reflected early political developments in relatively simple societies with limited suffrage rights, have been associated in recent times with high electoral polarization, adversarial politics, socially biased, minority governments, and policy instability. In contrast, multiparty systems, which result from widespread and continuing initiatives for policy and ideology innovation in democratic countries, are associated with inter-party competition and cooperation, broad public agendas, coalition governments with majority social support, consensual and relatively stable policy-making, and inclusive political institutions."

In today's diverse – but not divided – society, there is a greater demand for innovative policy solutions that take into account the differences in ideology voiced by a more disparate populace.

As the French sociologist Maurice Duverger discovered, a first-past-the-post voting system marginalizes third party representation and tends to result in a two-party system. Proportional representation through double ballot voting, on the other hand, eliminates the winner-take-all exclusion and creates a political atmosphere that favors multi-party participation.

Oddly enough, most countries with first-past-the-post elections for their bicameral legislature – otherwise called parliaments, not congresses – do have multi-party legislatures, unlike the United States' restrictive two-party system. Canada, the United Kingdom and India have consistently had multi-party parliaments and their proportional representation system of voting fosters third-party activity. Only in the U.S. has the two-party monopoly created legislation that effectively blocks third party representation.

Ironically, those legislated barriers to third party representation have alienated the voting public rather than strengthening the hold the two major parties intended to maintain over the electorate by implementing them.

A poll conducted by Pew Research in 2014, for instance, found that half of millennials no longer identified with either the Republican or the Democratic party. That was up from thirty-eight percent just ten years earlier. More importantly, thirty-one percent of millennials do not see any large difference between the policies of Republicans and Democrats.

The unfair influence of personal dynasties and the vested interests that support them within the two-party system has restricted the political dialogue in this country. It is only from the vigorous dialogue in a multi-party system that will come the innovative solutions to social problems that are now too often squelched or ignored by the two party's monopoly of our political system.

Without the divisive factionalism of a two-party system – that vicious "we're right, you're wrong" attitude and mentality – a political menu of options across a wide spectrum of possibilities can be offered. The resulting public discussion and constructive, not vindictive, criticism which will then be brought forth can break up the current log jam of narrow political options and limited solutions to the problems of today's diverse society.

That increase in voter participation and dialogue would affect more than just the generation of millennials, too. Many studies suggest that a switch from a two-party to a multi-party system in this country would result in an increase in voter turnout between nine and twelve percent across the boards. As voters find they can take part in a dialogue greater than that offered by today's two main parties, there would be a coincident rise in the feeling they could again control their own fate and voice their own moral stance rather than being forced to vote only for the narrow political solutions offered them by our two-party monopoly.

In an ideal world, the government acts as a mirror to the populace. First, it reflects the wishes of the citizens of the country, and then it reflects those wishes after they've been put into effect: a cleaner environment, a marketplace without undue restriction, a security from foreign threat or influence, acceptable taxation and a minimal inflation, a community where individual rights are protected and where quality education is available for all – all the day to day offshoots of the inalienable rights noted in the Declaration of Independence. How those wishes are put into effect may vary, but in a multiparty system all wishes are at least taken into account and represented by a political party.

The narrow frame of a two-party system is like one of those tall, thin mirrors in a circus fun house where everything is distorted, in this case by the will of too many self-serving politicians. One of those distortions reflects the sharp division it has created between people. Politicians and public alike get used to fighting the opposition party to achieve victory. Success is measured by which party is victorious, not by how much good is done for the broad public.

The mirror of a multi-party electorate would be more panoramic and would offer a clear reflection of a wide range of public opinion and elected politicians more interested in serving the public than in serving themselves.

In a multi-party system, voters would not only have

far more choices beyond the narrow polarity available in today's two-party system. Representative legislation would be passed through a coalition of parties able to quickly enact the desired legislation without having to wait for the next major election and for an "opposing" party, then voted in, to get their agenda done. There would be a fluidity and an immediacy to a multi-party system which would make it far more responsive to popular representation than the frequent gridlock we see in our government as our two major parties dig their heels in on issues and refuse to budge — their strategy only to be the "victorious" party, not to do the greatest good for their electorate.

The fact is that more parties mean more competition – an American principle – and that means the reduction of the unfair, narrow influence that the two predominant political parties in America have had…not to mention the curtailing of the oligarchic influence of those ingrained personal political dynasties.

More competition also means more motivation to fix things when they've gone wrong, more citizen involvement to do so, and more communal solidarity in working for the common good. There would be an increased recognition that we all do have a part to play, and that we now have a party within the broader political spectrum to represent our own individual moral stance. We don't have to vote for what now are either obsolete choices, or one of two "absolute," but opposed choices, or choices that do not offer a valid excitement about who or what is on the ballot. Those unappealing choices all lead to today's inactive voter turnout.

We don't have to be the effect of that divisive aspect of human nature that is now fostered by the oppositional politics of the two-party system.

We can have control again.

Chapter Six

"The happiness of society depends so much on preventing party spirit from infecting the common intercourse of life, that nothing should be spared to harmonize and amalgamate the two parties in social circles."

~ Thomas Jefferson, July 1801

PART OF REGAINING control of our political life is the recognition of one other aspect of "human nature," but one that is the polar opposite of the selfishness and greed the Founding Fathers feared in man. It is the innate moral sense of a man to recognize when things are seriously amiss and the bravery to then do something about it.

That moral sense was the motivation of the early American patriots to declare their independence by acting under the "Laws of Nature and of Nature's God." That moral sense is also the motivation for men today to support only those political agendas that do the greatest good for the greatest amount of people. Unfortunately, those political agendas are not easily available through our current two-party system. We need to change that.

We can start at the local level, move up to the state level and then finally concentrate our activities on the federal level.

There are five major barriers the two major parties have ensured are in place to protect their monopoly from any third party candidacies. Three of these barriers are more easily addressed and can be removed without a major change in government structure: campaign financing, balloting issues and debate entries. The other two barriers are more firmly embedded in the American political structure and would require a significant rearrangement of government structure: repeal of the Twelfth Amendment, if not the Electoral College itself, and the introduction of term limits to all congressional office holders.

Although these barriers to multi-party representation have become most obvious at the level of presidential elections, they also restrict state level campaigns. The unrestricted expansion of the federal government that began in 1913 with the ratification of the 16th and 17th Amendments also tended to snuff out the third parties that had recently become active and influential in the late nineteen hundreds and the early twentieth century Progressive Era when minority voices began to speak out about the freedoms they felt were denied them.

As the focus on national elections began to dominate the political scene after the 17th Amendment and the switch to a popular vote of senators, the public became less inclined to support single issue parties that often only had a local focus. At the same time, the two prominent national parties worked hard to co-opt or adopt these third party issues – at least in name – and so bring these view-points from broader, often morally based, political inter-ests into their own narrow, two-party monopoly. As they did, that monopoly became more pragmatic, more politi-cal, and less morally based itself.

The People's (or Populist) Party, the Socialist-Labor Party, the Prohibition Party, and a host of other farm relief, religious tolerance and social betterment parties all were subsumed into the Republican and Democratic platforms of the time. Their issues became diluted into what the two-party monopoly believed would be "acceptable," and therefore supportable, by voters. The voices of those seg-ments of the society who were now becoming aware that some of their inalienable human rights had been suffocat-ed in the harsh mechanisms of the Industrial Age could still not gain enough political traction through the third par-ties they formed on a national level. Although many third party candidates did become successful in state and lo-cal elections, the newly formed and financed Republican/ Democratic machines were still able to strengthen their stranglehold on "acceptable" policy at a national level.

The nineteen-sixties brought another period of loudly raised voices in support of morally based minority view-points – civil rights, women's movements, anti-war coali-tions, to name a few – but with no historical precedents for third party success, these voices were raised only in public protests, sit-ins and marches and relied on the media to broadcast their dissatisfaction. While they also had some success electing representative candidates at local levels, they were still effectively barred from national, alternative party representation despite the large constituencies their philosophies had.

The two major parties may have sometimes acknowledged the validity of their points of view, but these minorities were still effectively barred from the "acceptable" range of political representation.

Since World War II only billionaire Ross Perot has had enough personal funding to attempt to overcome the financial barriers that have effectively squashed third party candidacies since 1913. He was not successful, but he received nineteen percent of the popular vote, the most successful third party run since Teddy Roosevelt in 1912.

The current cost of running a presidential campaign is a separate issue, but at least those financial barriers to multi-party candidacies which have been put into place in the last fifty years can be removed. As the dual monopoly in American Politics, the Republicans and Democrats have passed legislation at the federal and state levels which keep alternative parties from receiving the funding needed to compete with candidates from either of the two main parties. These unfair financial restrictions have already been mentioned, but one other significant slap in the face was given to third parties by the Republican/Democratic monopoly in their 1974 "campaign reform" legislation.

This new law established the Presidential Election

Campaign Fund, which provided matching funds to eligible candidates when taxpayers assigned a small amount of their tax return on their 1040 form to finance the fund. However, to date only presidential candidates from our two main parties have received any matching funds. Per the law, third party candidates would only receive matching funds if they met the five percent vote criterion in the previous election, a criterion impossible to meet given the other financing, balloting and debate barriers.

The Presidential Election Campaign Fund may have been a public relations success initially, but it turned out to be as self serving and self-protective as the other barriers the two parties had erected. Today, having finally recognized this ruse, ninety-four percent of Americans have stopped checking off that 1040 form donation box.

Removing these arbitrary restrictions on alternative party financing would not only reduce the cost of today's presidential elections for alternative parties, it would also help free alternative parties up to receive private funding without the worry of their being stopped in their election tracks before they even leave the starting gate.

Removing the current balloting restrictions would also make the private funding of alternative party candidates more attractive if there were no longer such punitive restrictions on their even entering a national political race.

The League of Women Voters, a non-partisan public organization, had controlled the debate rules until 1987, but then the Commission of Presidential Debates, a non-profit corporation, was created by the two ruling parties,

Democrats and Republicans. Within a year the League had been pushed aside and only elected politicians could approve the debate monitors, could pre-approve the debate questions, and could influence the press not to ask follow up questions of the candidates.

In 1988 the League of Women Voters withdrew their sponsorship for the debates altogether because of the "secret" agreements being made about which candidates could participate and what questions could be asked. They claimed the debates had become "a fraud on the American voter" by the two predominant campaign organizations. The word "collusion" was not used, but the activity was implied.

No alternative candidate has even made it to the debates – unfair as they themselves might be – since 2000 because of those balloting restrictions the Commission on Presidential Debates has placed on candidates, in particular the requirement of a fifteen percent rating by a candidate in five national polls.

These arbitrary balloting restrictions only protect the Republican/Democrat monopoly. In order to give the American voting public the option to be represented by viable candidates, who represent the expanse of political views in today's diverse society, these balloting restrictions need to be de-legislated.

The Electoral College was originally created by the Founding Fathers to facilitate the administration of presidential and vice presidential elections without – yes, *without* – political parties and without national campaigns.

Ironically, the Twelfth Amendment ended up giving validation to the role of political parties in American presidential elections. This covert stamp of approval – legislated by politicians who had already become party defenders — quickly turned into the two-party monopoly we have had in the federal government ever since.

It is debatable if the Electoral College itself should be abolished, but the Twelfth Amendment will only be repealed if an intelligently conceived replacement system is proposed. A newly instituted, more fair, voting mechanism would keep open the possibility of multi-party elections and proportionate representation through a voting tally other than the current first-past-the-post system that eliminates formal representation by even the most strongly supported minority candidates.

Replacing or rewriting the 12th Amendment would be a long term, but important goal for establishing a more equitable and representative election format. So too would the placement of term limits on U.S. congressmen.

After World War II the 22nd Amendment placed term limits on presidencies. In doing so it restricted the power of personal dynasties in that office, but continued to allow the growth of personal dynasties in Congress. In fact, their greatest growth has been after the 22nd Amendment was ratified. Since then, the legislative branch of government has been able to hold a disproportionate amount of potential power in government with its expanding personal dynasties.

Congress today has the attraction of self-serving power

and wealth through building one's own personal dynasty, just as is done in other corporate or institutional careers. This caters to that more base human nature of man and can easily outweigh the more selfless motivation envisioned by the Founding Fathers to hold office. A two term limit would encourage those who run for Congress to act on a higher moral purpose for serving one's fellow countrymen in government.

Even Jefferson, first proponent of the two-party system, was aware of both the ethical and practical dangers of holding any political office too long. He wrote, "If some termination to the services of the chief magistrate be not fixed by the Constitution, or supplied by practice, his office, nominally for years, will in fact, become for life; and history shows how easily that degenerates into an inheritance."

How do we then return the office to candidates with that higher moral purpose, regardless if they are from the two leading parties or if they represent the wider, multi-party range of alternative political views?

Chapter Seven

"My country, right or wrong; if right, to be kept right, and if wrong, to be set right."

Carl Shurz, Secretary of the Interior,
Founder of Liberal Republican Party third party – 1872

HOW DO WE "set things right"?

Charles Schulz formed a third party to do so, but that was in the days when starting an alternative party was simple and straightforward.

With the collusion since WWII between mainstream Republicans and Democrats to bar third party runs, that is no longer possible. The "baneful effects" of party politics which George Washington warned us about are front and center, not only in today's divisive political culture, but in the embedded political dynasties behind that division.

The two-party system needs to go. That corruption needs reform.

But how? We cannot storm the Bastille. We cannot behead Marie Antoinette. We can, however, let people know, as Paul Revere did in his midnight ride, that the redcoats are coming. That, in fact, they're already here in these personal dynasties, although today those redcoats are all in Gucci or Armani garb.

There are things we can do immediately. We can promote a multi-party system in independent and social media. We can cancel the idea of a wasted vote by voting for a competent, moral third party candidate. We can politic our own Senators and Representatives, state and national, to eliminate the 12th Amendment or Electoral College. We can agitate to remove our individual state's punitive ballot laws. We can publicly push the need for congressional term limits.

With those actions we can begin to regain some measure of our own political control, just by speaking out. Educating others – both those in office and those on the street – is the first step to make others aware of the magnitude of how rigged our two-party system has become so they too can take their own first steps to set it right. It's a moral choice, a duty one has as a citizen, and comparable to the moral choice the Founding Fathers made by forming the country.

We are not going to reform this system solely by speaking out from the outside. Reform will have to be done from within the system. Those five barriers to a functioning multi-party system within the county have been legislated in by the two controlling parties.

They can therefore be legislated out.

By voting for candidates who favor getting rid of those

five barriers, and by ensuring state and federal legislatures are increasingly populated with those who wish to legislate some sanity back into our electoral system, we will ultimately effect the changes needed. It might not be by next Friday at noon, but it will come.

We can shift the country from the two-party republic it has become to the true democracy – with proportional representation and a multi-party system — that it should be.

We need to start electing progressive, moral, honest and selfless candidates who will vote to curb third party barriers and end the oligarchy of career politicians who are in office for the wrong reasons. We, as voters, are the ultimate check and balance of the American system, more powerful than the executive, judicial and certainly legislative branches of the government. Although the government may now be funded without restraint, we are the ultimate source of power behind those officials because without our vote, they would not be in office.

Government office holders have only been elected to represent us, and they should be beholden to selflessly representing the many points of view that make up our republic. We need to reestablish our own community over their corruption by promoting morality over politics, civility over absurdity, decency over division, equality over privilege, not just in government, but within ourselves, as responsible citizens, so that "we" do not end up destroying ourselves from within, as Lincoln warned.

We just need to rise and perch on the shoulders of those giants who preceded us, the Founding Fathers, and eliminate the two-party factionalism they so wisely warned us of.